Thoughts of a Wolf

Lissa Gromley

Published by Lissa Gromley, 2023.

THOUGHTS OF A WOLF

First edition. March 14, 2023.

ISBN: 979-8215153574

Written by Lissa Gromley.

Thoughts of a Wolf

An educational coloring book by Lissa Gromley.

Lissa Gromley has always loved wolves and dedicated half her life to learning about these marvelous creatures. All it took was looking at one photo of a wild wolf and her heart was set for life.

About this book

This coloring book was created with the love of wolves in mind. If you enjoy coloring and love wolves, while wanting to know what they may possibly think about, this book is for you. It is also for children of all ages. I am by no means a great artist, but drawing is one of my passions as is writing. I hope you will find this book enjoyable, as much as I did drawing each wolf. On some of the pages, there is an extra large space where you can draw your own wolf and then color it too! Have fun!

Lissa Gromley

Did you know that wolves have pups only around spring time? They are born blind and deaf. and rely on their mother for milk until the time she weans them. They can have litters anywhere from two to ten pups, but the usual number is about four to six pups. Wolf pups are always born dark. Even Arctic wolf pups are born dark and will lighten as they grow older. Did you know Black phase wolves will actually lighten as well? Nature is truly amazing!

Can you draw a

wolf pup?

Wolves are terrific swimmers! With their powerful legs, large paws, and narrow chests they can easily navigate the water, even being able to swim across an entire lake! Their double coat helps them to stay dry. After reaching land, they merely shake off the water from the top layers of their coat.

Can you draw a wolf swimming?

Wolves can dig very deep holes. Have you ever seen a groundhog hole? Imagine that hole to be ten times as wide and ten times as deep. A wolf's claws are strong enough to dig through even the hardest rocky ground. They may dig to make shelter or to find food. Sometimes wolves may dig just for fun or to lay down inside their holes just to rest. Sometimes they may hide within these holes as a form of self-defense.

Can you draw a wolf digging a hole?

Wolves love to roll in things they find pleasantly smelling that we humans would naturally find disgusting and stinky. They start with their faces first, rubbing their cheeks against the smelly object and then proceed to roll in it. This is called scent rolling. Speaking of scent, wolves will use their scent to mark their territory. This ensures that other wolf pack members know where the territory is and lets other traveling wolf packs know there is another wolf pack living there.

Can you draw a wolf scent-rolling in something?

Wolves are naturally shy creatures that will run and hide at the first sight of a human they don't know. Remember the saying, "Stranger danger?" This is how a wolf feels. When a wolf gets cornered, they may duck down with their tail between their legs and bare their fangs. This isn't aggression. They are just scared. Even so, a scared wolf may still bite. Always give a feared wolf respect and extra space. The best thing you can do is leave them alone when they are frightened. Never corner a wolf.

Can you draw a wolf that's afraid?

Wolves communicate through several different ways, but the most familiar to us is their howling. Their howls can be heard from miles away and can mean many things, from just being happy, to rallying a hunt, to letting another pack know not to come close, or to mourn the loss of a loved one.

They can howl any time of the day or night. Did you know that people used to think that wolves only howled at the moon and that some believed that it was a sign of an omen or a sign of evil?

Did you know that wolves also love to play? These animals enjoy a good romp and chase each other just for fun. Play time can be initiated by an act of the simple play bow, through expressive eyes, or just plain goofiness enticing other wolves to join in. Some of this playing can resemble fighting, but it's much more relaxed and of friendly nature.

Sometimes this playing can last for quite some time! The playing wolves always do their best to make sure no one is severely hurt. After playing, a wolf may rest for a bit before returning to play or before doing something else, such as hunting or exploring.

I like to roll
about while
looking at my
family to see if
they'll join in
with me.

Can you draw a wolf playing or resting after playing?

Wolves run for many reasons; for hunting and chasing down prey, to run from danger, or just for fun! Sometimes this running also involves a form of playing or even traveling. Wolves can run really fast, about 40 mph and they can run for hours before they become exhausted.

Can you draw a wolf running?

Wolf vs Husky

A wolf is very much different from a husky. A wolf will always have a larger head with a triangular shape with rounded ears that are well furred. A husky has a more rounded head with thin ears not so well furred. A wolf's muzzle is narrow while a husky's is short and broad. Wolves have yellow, brown, or green eyes. Huskies can have these varieties but some have blue.

Sometimes there may be a mix of various dog breeds that make it look so wolfy it can be mistaken for a wolf. Other identifying factors that can be mistaken for wolf content include, a sloped forehead; such as the collie's, long thin legs and splayed feet that can result in various mixed breeds of dogs. Most pure dogs have a stop, the area between their muzzle and forehead that causes your hand to pause before it goes up over the dog's head. A wolf has a little to minimal stop.

Did you know that blue eyes in a dog is a dog trait? No pure wolf ever has blue eyes. Wolves also have much larger paws that are less rounded than a dog's. The toes of a wolf are a little more spread apart between each other compared to a dog's toes.

Sometimes at a far distance, it is easy to mistake these animals for pure wolves or for having wolfdog content in them when the truth is they are just dogs with no wolf in them. Down below are some pictures of other dogs often confused for having some or all wolf in them.

Can you draw a wolf or a husky?

Shikoku Ken:
Fushiguro
Vanitas
100% dog
Owned by Aj
Sora Floyd

Angel:
Purebred
Siberian Husky.
Owned by Aly
Way.

Summer coat and Winter Coat

During the warm months, a wolf will have a much thinner look to themselves! This is because they molted (large amounts of shedding) to help keep their bodies cooler in the warmer months. In the winter time, this coat will double in size! Did you know wolves love winter? Between summer and winter, a wolf does far better in colder temperatures than in the warmer temperatures.

Can you draw a wolf in its summer coat?

How High Can A Wolf Jump?

Wolves are powerful jumpers. They can jump up to 12 feet high in a single leap! Unless there is some type of blockage a wolf will jump a high fence without a problem. They can even climb fences if they feel the urge to. This is why lean-in guards are put in place over the fencing to discourage the wolf from climbing up and over. A lean-in fence is a type of extra fence that connects to the original fencing, but curls down over into a U-like shape, extending a few feet from the top of the fence.

Can you draw a wolf jumping up high?

A Wolf's Hearing

Wolves have excellent hearing. They can hear sounds from miles away! Their hearing has a frequency between 25khz up to 80 khz. Their hearing allows them to track down prey or to run away from potential danger that may be up ahead before they can even see it! This excellent hearing comes in handy for wolves.

Can you draw a wolf listening to something?

Wolves can live almost anywhere, but mostly in mountains, forests, tundras, deserts such as the Middle East or the Arctic Circle. Wolves may live in caves or abandoned dens by other animals that they enlarge to fit inside. They may even use a hollowed out log.

Wolfdogs

Let's talk about wolfdogs. What is a wolfdog? A wolfdog has both wolf and dog in its genes. Which side shows more on the physical and behavioral traits depends on genetics. For example, if a wolfdog's genes display more wolf than dog so that we are not able to tell it from a pure wolf, the wolfdog would be a high-content. If they show half of each, they might be considered mid-content.

The more dog features coming through, they might be considered low-content. Down below are some pictures of wolfdogs of various contents that you can color, along with their photographs so you can see the differences between these beautiful animals.

Did you know there is a difference between a wolfdog and a wolf-hybrid? A wolfdog is always bred out of two wolfdogs where a wolf hybrid has one pure wolf parent and one pure dog parent.

Reaper Joe: Mid-content wolfdog owned by Brianna Jones.

Can you draw Reaper Joe?

Yicha: High-content wolfdog. Owned by Susan Vogt.

Rosemary: High
Content
Wolfdog
Owned by Lori
Wynn

A high content wolfdog looks nearly identical to a pure wolf, which can be confusing to some people who see one! I remember the first time I saw a high-content wolfdog that I actually thought was a pure wolf! I was educated that it is extremely rare for an ordinary person to own a pure wolf. In many places it is illegal to own a high-content wolfdog without a special type of permit. Did you know that some states/cities also require permits for all wolfdog contents?

Can you draw a high-content wolfdog?

Sage: Mid-content wolf   Owned by Lori Wynn   RIP Sage

A mid-content wolfdog can display traits from both a dog and a wolf. Sage was a former Ambassador of Guardians of the Wolves, a predecessor to Rosemary.

Can you draw Sage or another mid-content wolfdog?

Loki: Low/Mid
Content.
Owned by
Jared & Stacy
Lemert.

Dakota: Low/Mid-Content wolfdog owned by Jessica Wallace.

Sometimes a wolfdog may display physical characteristics of both low and mid, leaning more to one side than the other. This is where the DNA test Embark would come in handy to check to see if there is a bit of wolf or a little more wolf present in the dog's genes.

Can you draw Loki or another low/mid-content wolfdog?

Skyla: Low
Content
Wolfdog.
Owned by
Heather Ross.

Low-Content
wolfdog.
Owned by:
Annika Helms

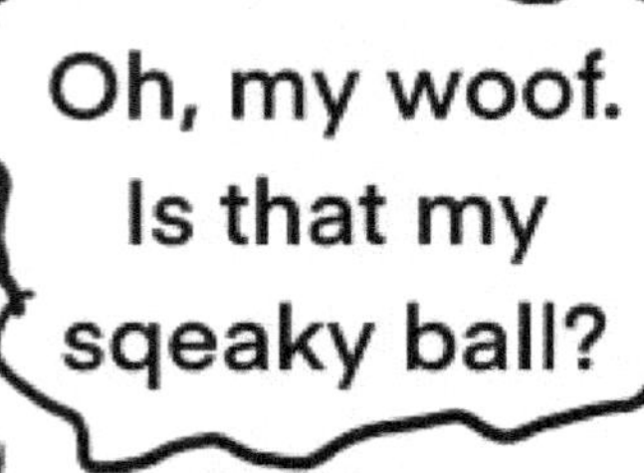

Cloud Inuyasha
Strife: Low-
Content
wolfdog.
Owned by Aj
Sora Floyd

A low content displays very little wolf content, but there are some low-contents that can look pretty wolfy, including dogs with nothing but dog breeds in its DNA, which can get pretty confusing! In cases like this, it is best to have a DNA test to check if there are any wolf genes.

Can you draw a low-content wolfdog?

Luna: Low-
Content.
Owned by
Jared & Stacy
Lemert.

Karma: Low-Content Wolfdog. Owned by Alisha Donovan

Wolfdog Puppies

Wolfdog puppies! They're adorable, quirky, and a lot of work! Did you know that it's sometimes impossible to tell a high-content wolfdog puppy from a low-content wolf-dog puppy except for varying factors, such as darkened fur and time of birth?

Like pure wolves, high-content wolfdog puppies are born only in the springtime. Because some lower-contents and regular dog puppies can be born in the springtime too, it is best to use a DNA test to tell just how much wolf there is, if any. This is because puppies of varying contents can look similar to each other until they grow older.

Down below are drawings of wolfdog puppies graciously provided by their owners to be included within this book for you to color.

Kronos: Low-content wolfdog puppy owned by Kat Breitling.

Lupa: Low-content wolfdog puppy owned by Victoria Joseph Hasty.

Rosemary:
High-Content
wolfdog puppy
Owned by Lori
Wynn.

Can you draw Kronos, Lupa, or Rosemary as puppies?

Willow: High-Content Wolfdog puppy. Owned by Lori Wynn.

Luna: Low-Content Wolfdog puppy owned by Jared&Stacy Lemert.

Loki: Low/Mid Content Wolfdog puppy owned by Jared&Stacy Lemert.

Tehya: High-Content wolfdog puppy owned by Tim Cartrett.

Kitchi: High-
content
wolfdog puppy
owned by Tim
Cartrett

Karma: Low-content wolfdog puppy owned by Alisha Donovan.

Nyala: Low-content wolfdog puppy owned by Jessica Hatley.

Shontonga Min: Uppermid-Content wolfdog puppy owned by Jason Ogg.

Blade: Low-content wolfdog puppy owned by April Keaton.

Kuvira: Low-content wolfdog puppy owned by Aj Sora Floyd.

Yicha: High-content wolfdog puppy owned by Susan Vogt.

Nancy: Mid-content wolfdog puppy owned by Susan Vogt.

Kita: Low-content wolfdog puppy owned by Sky Taylor.

Kei: Low-content wolfdog puppy owned by Sky Taylor.

Woofers in Cosplay

Some wolfdog owners enjoy dressing their woofers up for the holidays with their woofers taking it really well! As well as one can expect! It can be fun to dress up a woofer, especially when the woofer enjoys it as much as their fur-parent. Advisable, it is best to start them young when introducing them to clothing and costumes. If a wolfdog does not like it, it should never be forced on them. It's less fun that way for everyone involved. Down below there are some pictures of wolfdogs in costumes to color.

Can you draw a wolfdog or dog in your favorite costume?

Photo by Lori Wynn.

Photo by Aj Sora Floyd.

Is there wolf-content?

Sometimes, it can be difficult to accurately guess if there is wolf content in a dog. This is why it is best to use Embark, the DNA test that will accurately inform you of any wolf content. Embark will say "grey wolf" as part of the mix if there is any. It will never say Timber wolf, Mexican wolf, or Arctic wolf; sub-species of the grey wolf. Be wary of breeders who try to sell puppies, especially all white ones or reddish brown ones claiming that their pups have these wolf subspecies in them.

Spirit: Unknown
content
owned by
Susan Sayers.

This coloring book is dedicated to a very special woofer who left this world too soon, leaving many hearts broken and many tears shed. Faelen will always be in the hearts of the wolfdog community and we stand by Phil Young's side as a support system.

In memory of Faelen owned by Phil Young.

More wolves to color

You can learn
more about
wolves and
wolfdogs
through
educational
programs such
as Guardians of
the Wolves.

Thank you for
your support!

Acknowledgements

This coloring book was inspired by the many people who made the wolfdog community a better place. I wish to express my sincere thanks and gratitude to all of those who graciously submitted photos of their wolfdogs and dogs to be included within this coloring book for educational learning and fun. Special thanks goes to Guardians of the Wolves for being a big supporter of this project.

www.ingramcontent.com/pod-product-compliance
Lightning Source LLC
Chambersburg PA
CBHW081407130726
47998CB00011B/3097